The INSIDE GUIDE

GLOBAL GEOGRAPHY

Exploring the Geography of Russia and Its Neighbors

By Heather Smore

Cavendish Square

Published in 2026 by Cavendish Square Publishing, LLC
2544 Clinton Street Buffalo, NY 14224

Website: cavendishsq.com

Disclaimer: Portions of this work were originally authored by Ryan Wolf and published as *The Geography of Russia and the Eurasian Republics* (Explore the World). All new material this edition authored by Heather Smore.

All websites were available and accurate when this book was sent to press.

Cataloging-in-Publication Data

Names: Smore, Heather.
Title: Exploring the geography of Russia and its neighbors / Heather Smore.
Description: Buffalo, NY : Cavendish Square Publishing, 2026. | Series: The inside guide: global geography | Includes glossary and index.
Identifiers: ISBN 9781502674227 (pbk.) | ISBN 9781502674234 (library bound) | ISBN 9781502674241 (ebook)
Subjects: LCSH: Russia (Federation)–Geography–Juvenile literature. | Russia (Federation)–Juvenile literature.
Classification: LCC DK510.28 S66 2026 | DDC 914.7–dc23

Editor: Katie Kawa
Designer: Deanna Lepovich

The photographs in this book are used by permission and through the courtesy of: Cover Alexey Oblov/Shutterstock.com; p. 4 Dimitrios Karamitros/Shutterstock.com; p. 6 Vladimir Lugai/Shutterstock.com; p. 7 Drop of Light/Shutterstock.com; p. 8 (top) olgadiukareva/Shutterstock.com; p. 8 (bottom) gluuker/Shutterstock.com; p. 9 MaxZolotukhin/Shutterstock.com; p. 10 Ondrej Prosicky/Shutterstock.com; p. 12 (top) Yakov Oskanov/Shutterstock.com; p. 12 (bottom) Stanislav Duben/Shutterstock.com; p. 13 Shchipkova Elena/Shutterstock.com; p. 14 Dmitrii_Smirnov/Shutterstock.com; p. 15 Piu_Piu/Shutterstock.com; p. 16 Deman/Shutterstock.com; p. 18 Olga Rolenko/Shutterstock.com; p. 19 BEST-BACKGROUNDS/Shutterstock.com; p. 20 NOWAK LUKASZ/Shutterstock.com; p. 21 7ynp100/Shutterstock.com; p. 22 kibri_ho/Shutterstock.com; p. 24 volkova natalia/Shutterstock.com; p. 25 ZekeriyaSen/Shutterstock.com; p. 26 magnetix/Shutterstock.com; p. 27 Artem Dunkel/Shutterstock.com; p. 28 (graphic organizer) Fireofheart/Shutterstock.com; p. 28 (top left and center) Oasis World/Shutterstock.com; p. 28 (top right) Katty2016/Shutterstock.com; p. 28 (bottom left) Extezy/Shutterstock.com; p. 28 (bottom right) Peter Hermes Furian/Shutterstock.com; p. 29 (left) Catarina Belova/Shutterstock.com; p. 29 (right) ChocoPie/Shutterstock.com.

CPSIA compliance information: Batch #CSCSQ26: For further information contact Cavendish Square Publishing LLC at 1-877-980-4450.

Printed in the United States of America

CONTENTS

Russia has controlled a large area of the Eurasian landmass throughout history. Today, areas that were once under Russia's control are now its independent neighbors, as shown on this map.

A CHANGING LANDSCAPE

Chapter One

Stretching into Europe and Asia, Russia is a very large nation that has had a lot of influence on the lands surrounding it throughout history. The borders of Russia and its neighboring nations have shifted over time. Wars, revolutions, and migrations often changed where humans drew the lines between countries. New nations were formed and became independent, changing world maps time and again. Today, this region is still dealing with changes to its geography and national boundaries due to the actions of humans and their governments.

Fast Fact

Russia and its neighbors are part of the Eurasian landmass, which includes the continents of Europe and Asia. Russia is both a European and an Asian country, with lands that reach across both continents.

A Large and Powerful Nation

Russia is not just the largest country on the Eurasian landmass—it's the largest country on Earth. This nation covers more than 6.6 million square miles (17.1 million sq km), running from the edges of Europe to the far eastern part of Asia. At one point, Russia's lands stretched as far as

The Ural Mountains (*shown here*) run through Russia. Geographers use these mountains as a boundary between Europe and Asia.

Alaska in North America. However, Russia sold its Alaskan territory to the United States in 1867.

Because of its size, Russia often dominated its neighbors—sometimes bringing them under its control. In the 1990s, though, many of the territories controlled by Russia broke away to form their own separate nations.

Russia Today

Today, Russia is broken up into more than 80 political divisions, each with their own local governments. There are oblasts, which are similar to U.S. states, and other special areas. These all come together to form the Russian Federation.

Fast Fact

Russia borders many other nations, including China, Mongolia, and Finland. Its longest border is the one it shares with Kazakhstan, and its shortest border is shared with North Korea.

THE SOVIET UNION

Russia and its neighbors were once part of the Union of Soviet Socialist Republics (USSR), also known as the Soviet Union. This was a group of states controlled by Russia from 1922 to 1991. During this period, the powerful Soviet government claimed it was dedicated to the common people. In reality, its policies led to the deaths of more than 20 million citizens from starvation and state-inflicted violence.

When the Soviet Union broke apart in 1991, its former territories became self-ruling republics that did not have to serve the Russian government. However, Russia remains a powerful—and sometimes **aggressive**—political and military force in the region.

In recent years, Russia has taken control of lands that once belonged to its independent neighbors. In 2014, it seized, or took over, the Crimean **Peninsula** in Ukraine. Then, in 2022, Russian troops invaded Ukraine, starting a war that has led to many deaths and damage to buildings, such as the ones shown here.

Russia borders several bodies of water, including the Arctic Ocean to the north, the Pacific Ocean to the east, and the Black Sea (*shown here*) to the west.

Fast Fact

Because of its size, Russia has 11 different time zones. When it is midnight in Moscow, it is 7 a.m. in Vladivostok!

Most Russians live to the west of the Ural Mountains in what is considered Europe, in cities such as Moscow and Saint Petersburg. Large populations are also found in Asian cities such as Novosibirsk and Omsk, and in Vladivostok on the Pacific coast. Much of the country is **uninhabited** due to its bitterly cold climate.

Eastern European Nations

Many of Russia's neighbors are located in Eastern Europe. After the Soviet Union's end in 1991, newly independent republics located in Eastern Europe included Moldova, Belarus, and Ukraine. Even under Russian control, these areas maintained their own

Eastern European nations are home to many beautiful historic buildings, such as these in Belarus. This region has a rich history and is home to many unique, or special, sites.

traditions, **cultures**, and languages, which have flourished in their new **era** of independence.

At the same time, the Baltic states of Lithuania, Latvia, and Estonia also declared their independence. These nations sit beside the Baltic Sea. Today, they are part of the European Union (EU), which is a political and economic union of more than 20 European nations.

Central Asian Countries

Many parts of Central Asia also became independent nations after the fall of the Soviet Union. Some, such as Kyrgyzstan and Tajikistan, have mostly Muslim populations. Kazakhstan is the largest of Russia's neighbors and the largest landlocked nation in the world. Uzbekistan contains cities important to the history of Muslim culture, while Turkmenistan is mostly covered by the Karakum Desert.

Some Asian nations sit south of Russia within the Caucasus Mountains, nestled between the Black and Caspian Seas. Armenia and Azerbaijan are located in these mountains. Another country found there is Georgia, which is located on the border of Europe and Asia.

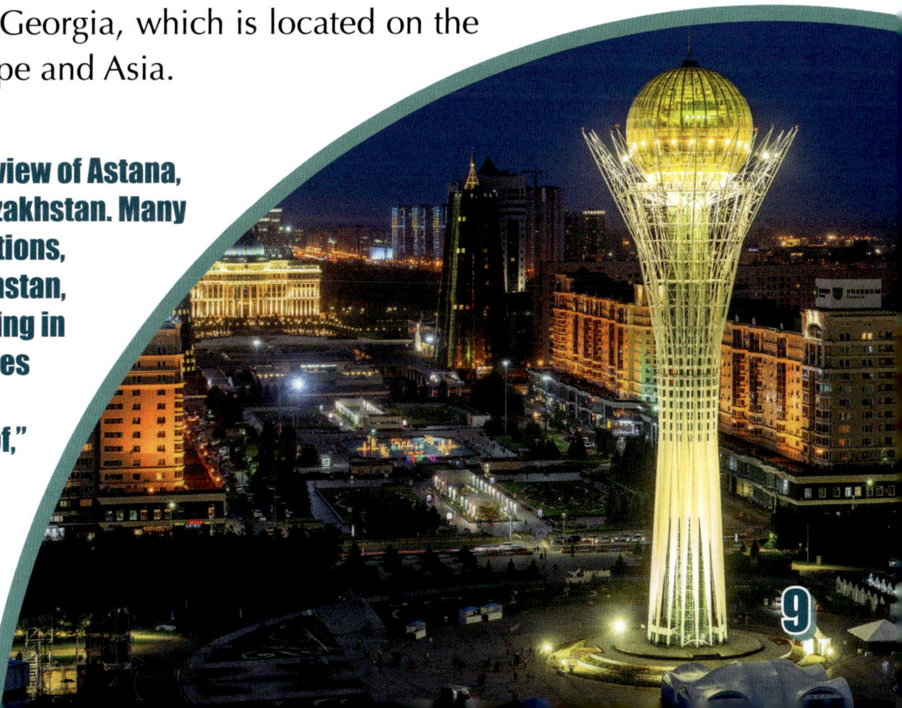

Shown here is a view of Astana, the capital of Kazakhstan. Many Central Asian nations, including Kazakhstan, have names ending in "-stan." This comes from the Persian word for "place of," so Kazakhstan means "place of the Kazakhs."

The many biomes of Russia and its neighboring nations are home to a wide variety of plants and animals, including bears such as the one shown here.

BEAUTIFUL BIOMES

Chapter Two

Biomes are geographic areas defined by the animal and plant life they share. Russia and its neighbors have many biomes, each with their own unique climates and natural features. The landforms, bodies of water, wildlife, and natural resources found in these diverse places have a major impact on the people who live there.

Studying the Steppe

The Eurasian steppe is a long belt of grasslands that sweeps from the eastern European plain into the heart of Central Asia. The steppe begins in Hungary and includes southern Ukraine and Russia, much of Kazakhstan, and parts of Mongolia and China. The sprawling grasslands end at the feet of various mountain ranges, forests, and deserts.

With few trees in sight, the land offers little shelter for those passing through. The dry soil in this grassland biome makes it a difficult area for farming. However, many animals graze along the steppe, enjoying the diverse species of grass found there.

Fast Fact

Humans first **domesticated** wild horses for use in transportation and warfare in parts of the Eurasian steppe.

The saiga antelope lives in areas of the Eurasian steppe, especially in Russia and Kazakhstan. Hunting has put these creatures in danger of extinction, or dying out.

Fast Fact

The Eurasian steppe is split by Central Asia's Altai Mountains. The eastern steppe region has more extreme summer and winter weather than the western steppe.

A Forest Biome

The world's largest land biome stretches across Russia, as well as many other parts of Europe and North America. It is a forest dominated by coniferous evergreen trees that spread by dropping cones containing their seeds. This biome is known as the taiga, or boreal forest.

The majority of Russia falls within the taiga biome. Common evergreen trees in the taiga include the larch, fir, pine, and spruce. The taiga features a variety of wildlife, including

These young Siberian tigers are playing in the snow. The taiga gets around 20 to 40 inches (50.8 to 101.6 cm) of snow each year.

moose, elk, lynx, roe deer, gray wolves, red foxes, sables, brown bears, and the endangered Siberian tiger.

The Frozen Tundra

North of the taiga is a biome known as the tundra. The tundra is a cold, desert-like biome located near and inside the Arctic Circle. Much of northern Russia is composed of tundra zones that experience eight months of winter.

Beneath the frozen soil, known as permafrost, the tundra is filled with natural resources, such as oil. This biome is also home to a variety of large mammals and birds. Wildlife in northern Russia includes tundra wolves, polar bears, Arctic foxes, snowy owls, musk oxen, and

Fast Fact

Temperatures in the tundra biome of Russia have dropped as low as low as -90 degrees Fahrenheit (-68 degrees Celsius)!

Reindeer can be found in Russia's tundra biome. Some Indigenous, or Native, groups of the tundra, such as the Nenets (*shown here*), herd reindeer as part of their culture.

caribou. The Arctic waters north of the tundra are home to walruses and many kinds of whales.

What Is Siberia?

When people think of Siberia, they often think of the tundra. This is not completely correct, though. Siberia is a huge geographic region that stretches from the top of Russia down to Kazakhstan. It includes steppe, taiga, and tundra biomes. The Siberian tundra is in the far north of Russia, inside the Arctic Circle.

Siberia begins at the Ural Mountains in the west, ending at the Pacific Ocean. Most of Siberia is divided into the West Siberian Plain and the Central Siberian **Plateau**. The region's three major rivers, the Lena, the Ob, and the Yenisey, flow into the Arctic Ocean.

Siberia is more than just snowy stretches of empty land. It includes many biomes and covers the entire region of northern Asia.

OCEAN BIOMES

Russia and its neighbors are home to more than just land biomes. This part of the world also has access to major bodies of water, so the ocean biome is also part of the geography of this region.

The Arctic Ocean meets northern Russia at bodies of water such as the Barents, the Kara, the Laptev, and the East Siberian Seas. In addition, the Pacific Ocean touches Russia's eastern shores. These oceans are home to many unique species of fish and other sea creatures.

The Barents Sea (*shown here*) is changing due to global warming. The sea ice is melting, which will lead to changes for the animals that live in or near these waters, as well as changes in the weather in Russia and other European countries.

Minerals are one example of the many natural resources found in Russia and its neighbors in Eastern Europe and Asia. Mines, such as the one shown here in Russia, are places where minerals are extracted, or taken, from the earth.

Chapter Three

THE GIFTS OF GEOGRAPHY

Natural resources are an important part of a region's geography. They determine what kinds of industries can develop, where people settle, and how self-sufficient a country can be. Russia and its neighbors are rich in natural resources, with Russia having a wide variety of them due to its large size. These resources have supported the people of this region throughout its history, but their use—and often overuse—has caused problems for the environment, or natural world, as well.

Fossil Fuels and Minerals

Fossil fuels make up a large percentage of all Russian exports, or things it sells. Russia is one of the world's leaders in coal production. It is also the third-largest producer of oil and a major supplier of natural gas.

Additionally, Russia produces some of the highest amounts of gold, silver, and platinum in the world. On the Kamchatka Peninsula in northeastern Russia, a ring of volcanoes has also created deposits of rare minerals. Other countries in this region are

Fast Fact

As much as 13 percent of the world's oil may be located beneath the Arctic Ocean.

Shown here is an oil field in Siberia. This is a location where oil is taken from the ground. Russia has many oil fields on its lands and in the waters surrounding it.

also rich in mineral resources. For example, Kazakhstan has more uranium mines than any other country. Uranium is used to generate **nuclear energy**.

Important Waterways

Water is an extremely important natural resource. **Access** to water allows for transportation and the ability to support agriculture. In addition, people need clean freshwater resources for drinking, washing, and preparing food.

Russia and its neighbors have access to many major bodies of water, including the Pacific Ocean, Arctic Ocean, Baltic Sea, Black Sea, and Caspian Sea. In addition, one of the world's longest rivers—the Yenisey—flows through Russia. Other important rivers

Fast Fact

Lake Baikal, which is located in Russia, is the deepest lake in the world.

A SHRINKING SEA

Humans need water to survive, but sometimes the process of getting water causes more harm than good. The Aral Sea in Kazakhstan and Uzbekistan once was one of the world's largest lakes. During the 1960s, the Soviet Union diverted its water in order to turn the nearby desert into farmland. During the **irrigation** process, the sea lost more than half its size. This destroyed the local fishing industry. The dry basin left behind also created dust storms. The salty dust mixed with farm chemicals, which polluted the area. Today, the shrinking of the Aral Sea is considered an environmental disaster and a reminder of what can happen when humans interfere with nature.

This is what the Caspian Sea looks like from space. It is the world's largest inland body of water and is known for its oil reserves and fishing industry.

in this region include the Volga and the Ob.

Major Mountain Ranges

Mountain ranges are often home to natural resources, especially minerals, and there are many mountains in

The Pamir Mountains, shown here, are found mostly in the Central Asian nation of Tajikistan.

Fast Fact

Found in the Armenian highlands and visible from the Armenian capital of Yerevan, Mount Ararat is considered a national symbol by many Armenians, although it is located in Türkiye. Some Armenians see it as a reminder of the losses they suffered at the hands of the Turkish military during the 1915 to 1916 Armenian **genocide**.

Russia and its surrounding countries. The highest peak in the region is found in the Pamir mountain range. Ismoil Somoni, a mountain peak in Tajikistan, stands 24,590 feet (7,495 m) above sea level.

Other major mountain ranges in the region include the Ural Mountains, which divide Eurasia, and the Caucasus Mountains, which are home to the highest peak in Europe—Mount Elbrus, which is located in Russia.

The Era of Industrialization

The wealth of natural resources in this region fueled a period of industrialization that continues through modern times. Industrialization happens when a country or a region moves from having an economy focused on farming to one focused on the production of goods in factories. It is often brought about by changes in technology and the ability to use natural resources to power new machines.

Industrialization in the Soviet Union greatly altered the region's approach to its land. Mining, drilling, and large-scale farming supported the economy but endangered the environment. This is an important example of the powerful impact humans have on their geography.

The natural resources in this region are being used up more quickly than they can be replaced. In addition, pollution from factories, cars, and cities is contributing to the decrease in some resources, such as clean water.

The war between Russia and Ukraine has changed the landscape of this region in major ways.

AN UNCERTAIN FUTURE

Chapter Four

Russia and the lands surrounding it in Eastern Europe and Asia make up a region that is always changing. From the shifting borders following the breakup of the Soviet Union to wars in both the past and present, humans have shaped the geography of this region and continue to do so.

Climate change is also causing major shifts in this region, as weather patterns and resource availability become more **unpredictable**. Although it is hard to know what the future of this region will look like, one thing is certain—it will be shaped by the people who lead it and live in it.

The Growth of Cities

As the economy of this region shifted away from small-scale farming, more people moved to its cities, which have become major political, financial, and cultural centers. Cities central to the culture of Russia include Moscow, Omsk, and Saint Petersburg. As the Russian

Fast Fact

Many Central Asian cities are famous for their beautiful mosques. A mosque is a place where Muslims gather together to pray.

capital, Moscow is home to the Kremlin, which is the seat of the Russian government.

The cultures of Russia's neighbors are reflected in cities such as Kyiv, the capital of Ukraine, and Minsk, the capital of Belarus. Uzbekistan's capital of Tashkent is well known for its mosques, markets, and monuments. Almaty, the largest city in Kazakhstan, is one of Central Asia's historical and cultural centers.

Fast Fact

Moscow is where the leader of Russia, Vladimir Putin, lives. He is technically the country's president, but many people refer to him as a dictator, or someone who rules with absolute power.

Moscow (*shown here*) is Russia's most populated city. More than 13 million people live in this capital.

Getting Around the Region

The area covered by Russia and its neighboring nations is so large that major transportation systems needed to be developed to make getting around easier. Railroads, federal highways, and airports all bring people across miles of steppe, taiga, and tundra. Rivers, canals, and seas are also used for transportation and shipping.

Creating transportation systems has had a major impact on the environment. Clearing lands for railroad tracks and roads calls for the cutting down of many trees. Canals change natural waterways. Air travel and cars emit fossil fuels that contribute to climate change.

A Place of Power

Russia's geography has allowed it to protect itself throughout history. With its large stretches of land with extremely cold winters, Russia was very difficult to conquer. It grew in strength by taking over neighboring territories, increasing its size and becoming a major world power.

Fast Fact

The Trans-Siberian Railway is the longest railway in the world.

The Trans-Siberian Railway (*shown here*) moves people and goods across Russia, beginning in Moscow and ending in Vladivostok.

CLIMATE CHANGE CONCERNS

One of the biggest concerns in every part of the world today is climate change. The burning of fossil fuels for power puts gases in the air that trap heat from the sun. This plays a part in global warming, which can be a natural process of Earth's temperature going up over time but has sped up due to human activities. The increase in Earth's temperature causes climate change, with more extreme weather events such as floods, droughts, and storms.

In Russia and its neighboring countries, climate change has led to increased wildfires, heat waves, and precipitation.

Climate change is causing permafrost (*shown here*) to melt. This can cause problems for the living things that make their homes in the tundra. It can also cause the soil to get into waterways, polluting freshwater sources and making people sick.

The desire for geographic expansion is at the root of many of the political and military struggles Russia has had with its neighbors, including Ukraine. These issues may continue to affect borders in the future. In addition, war shapes the land in physical ways, destroying cities, farmland, and natural wonders.

Respecting the Land

People shape the land, but the land also shapes how people live. Geography has influenced how Russia and its neighbors developed over time, and the land continues to impact the economic, political, and cultural life of the people of this region.

Whether building cities beside rivers and lakes, mining within the mountains, or cutting timber in the taiga, humans have modified their physical environments to survive and prosper. As populations grow and the climate changes, Russia and its neighbors may need to adapt to their surroundings in new ways, respecting the land around them and working to preserve it for future generations.

Working to take care of the natural world and its beautiful geographic features is one way to build a better future—not just in this region, but also around the world.

RUSSIA AND ITS NEIGHBORS BY THE NUMBERS

Largest Country (by Area)

Russia: 6.6 million square miles (17.1 million sq km)

Most Populated Country

Russia: 146 million people

Smallest Country (by Area)

Armenia: 11,484 square miles (29,743 sq km)

Highest Point

Ismoil Somoni: 24,590 feet (7,495 m)

Longest River

Yenisey: 3,442 miles (5,540 km)

Note: Different sources report different lengths based on the inclusion or exclusion of tributaries, or branches of the river.

THINK ABOUT IT!

1. What part do you think geography played in the creation and the breakup of the Soviet Union?
2. Why do you think Russia has been able to remain the most powerful country in its part of the world for so many years?
3. What effects do you think Russia's war with Ukraine will have on the geography of this region?
4. How could Russia and its neighbors fight climate change?

GLOSSARY

access: The ability to use or enter something.

aggressive: Showing a readiness to attack.

culture: The beliefs and ways of life of a certain group of people.

domesticate: To breed and raise an animal for use by people.

era: A period of time beginning with some special date or event.

fossil fuel: A fuel—such as coal, oil, or natural gas—that is formed in the earth from dead plants or animals.

genocide: The purposeful and systematic destruction of a racial, political, or cultural group.

irrigation: The supplying of water to land by man-made means.

nuclear energy: Power created by splitting the nuclei, or center, of atoms.

peninsula: A piece of land surrounded by water on three sides.

plateau: A broad, flat area of high land.

uninhabited: Not occupied or lived in by people.

unpredictable: Tending to behave in ways that cannot be known or planned for ahead of time.

FIND OUT MORE

Books

Klepeis, Alicia. *Ukraine*. Minneapolis, MN: Bellwether Media, 2021.

Layton, Christine. *Travel to Russia*. Minneapolis, MN: Lerner Publications, 2022.

Marshall, Deb. *Russia*. New York, NY: Lightbox Learning, Inc., 2023.

Websites

BBC Bitesize: Introduction to Russia
www.bbc.co.uk/bitesize/articles/zcrx2v4
This website offers visitors a closer look at Russia, with videos, maps, and photos.

***National Geographic Kids*: Russia**
kids.nationalgeographic.com/geography/countries/article/russia
Visitors to this website can find a detailed overview of Russia's geography, history, and people.

UNICEF Youth: The War in Ukraine
www.unicef.org.au/unicef-youth/making-sense-of-emergencies/war-in-ukraine
This website, which was created by the children's organization UNICEF, aims to explain the conflict between Russia and Ukraine in a way that young people can understand.

Publisher's note to educators and parents: Our editors have carefully reviewed these websites to ensure that they are suitable for students. Many websites change frequently, however, and we cannot guarantee that a site's future contents will continue to meet our high standards of quality and educational value. Be advised that students should be closely supervised whenever they access the internet.

INDEX